How the Rich Make Their Money

Logan Evans

Copyright Page

First edition
All Rights Reserved
Author: © 2024, Logan Evans

Index

The Long Game Mentality

The long game mentality is what distinguishes millionaires from those who are simply looking to make a quick buck. They don't see their businesses as a way to solve their immediate needs, but rather as a tool to build a solid and sustainable future. Understanding this is crucial if you want to think like them. While most people are looking for quick results, millionaires focus on what they can achieve in five, ten, or even twenty years. It's like planting a tree: at first, you barely see any results, but over time it grows, gives shade and fruits.

For millionaires, every decision they make is designed with the long term in mind. They are not concerned with the immediate success of a project, but rather its long-term impact and potential. Imagine someone who decides to open a business. An ordinary person might worry if they don't make a huge profit in the first few months. However, a millionaire knows that the first few months or even the first few years are just one part of a bigger plan. Instead of despairing, they invest their time and resources into improving, learning, and building a solid foundation. They know that patience and consistency always pay off.

A key part of this mindset is understanding that money is not an end, but a means. Millionaires don't seek to get rich by spending it on superficial things. They constantly reinvest their money. Every dollar they earn is a seed they replant to grow even more. This means that even when they earn a lot, they don't spend mindlessly. They see money as energy that can be used to create more opportunities. This approach allows them to accumulate wealth while others lose it because they don't think about tomorrow.

Another important aspect is how they deal with failures. Millionaires don't see them as the end of the road, but as lessons. In the long game, failures are inevitable. It's like stumbling while walking down a long road. You don't stop or abandon the path; you just get up, analyze what went wrong, and continue. Each stumble makes them wiser and stronger. They know that success doesn't come overnight, but from the accumulation of small achievements and learning from mistakes.

An example of this mindset is how they view relationship building. For them, connections aren't just about what someone can offer them today, but what can emerge in the future. They invest time in getting to know people, building trust, and establishing genuine bonds. They understand that these relationships can open unexpected doors at the most needed times. It's like sowing friendship and loyalty to reap alliances when the time is right.

Furthermore, millionaires focus on creating businesses that can survive without them. They know that time is their most valuable resource, so they build systems and teams that can function independently of their daily presence. This frees up time to explore new ideas and opportunities, while always keeping their eyes on the horizon. They understand that to win in the long game, they need to delegate, trust, and build resilient structures.

It's important to note that this mindset doesn't mean being passive or just waiting. On the contrary, millionaires are extremely active in building their future. They work with discipline every day, but their effort is focused on lasting results. They aren't distracted by fads or opportunities that promise a lot but have no solid foundation. Their ability to say "no" to things that don't fit into their long-term vision is one of their greatest strengths.

The long-game mentality also leads them to invest in themselves. For them, learning never ends. They constantly seek out new skills, knowledge, and experiences that can enhance their capabilities. They see personal growth as one of the most valuable investments they can make. This not only helps them meet the challenges of the present, but prepares them to take advantage of the opportunities of the future.

In the end, what really defines millionaires is their ability to resist the temptation of instant gratification. While others spend on immediate luxuries or seek quick results, they stay focused on building something bigger, stronger, and longer lasting. This approach puts them in an advantageous position, because while others are busy chasing immediate success, they are already building their empire. Their patience, discipline, and long-term vision are the keys to their success. If you want to think like a millionaire, start seeing every action as an investment in your future and remember that great results take time.

The Power of Strategy

The power of strategy is what separates those who merely survive in business from those who thrive and achieve success. For millionaires, every move is calculated, every action has a purpose, and every decision is part of a larger plan. It's not about acting on instinct or winging it; it's about building a clear path and following it with determination. They understand that success doesn't just happen by chance, but is the direct result of a well-designed strategy.

Strategy is like a map. Before starting any business, millionaires make sure they know where they want to go and how they plan to get there. They don't start building without clear blueprints. They first identify their goal: it could be dominating a market, solving a specific problem, or creating a brand that is globally recognized. Once they have that goal, they lay out a detailed plan that includes every step necessary to achieve it. This plan not only gives them direction, but it also allows them to avoid common mistakes that others make when they are unprepared.

The interesting thing about the millionaires' strategy is that it doesn't just focus on what they have to do, but also on what they shouldn't do. They know that not every opportunity is a good one and that saying "no" to things that don't fit into their plan is just as important as saying "yes" to the right ones. This selective approach allows them to concentrate on what really matters and avoid spreading themselves thin across too many projects or ideas.

Furthermore, their strategy always includes an analysis of the environment. Millionaires study their market thoroughly before making any move. They ask themselves who their competitors are, what problems their customers face, and what trends are booming. They leave nothing to chance. This knowledge allows them to position themselves strategically, offering something unique or better than what already exists. They don't try to compete simply for the sake of competing; they seek to differentiate themselves and provide clear value that makes them stand out.

A key element of strategy is flexibility. While millionaires have a clear plan, they are also prepared to adapt if circumstances change. They are not stubborn to the point of following a path that clearly isn't working. If they see that something isn't working, they adjust their approach and look for new solutions. This doesn't mean abandoning their vision, but finding smarter ways to get there. It's like sailing a ship: if the currents change, they don't abandon the destination, they just adjust the sails.

Strategy also allows them to calculate risks. Unlike many people who are afraid to take risks, millionaires understand that risks are necessary for growth, but they don't take blind risks. They analyze each decision carefully, weighing the potential gains against the potential losses. If a risk has more benefits than drawbacks and fits into their overall strategy, they take it without hesitation. This calculated approach is what allows them to move forward while others are paralyzed by fear.

Another key aspect is execution. A strategy is worthless if it is not carried out. Millionaires are disciplined when it comes to implementing their plans. They make sure that every action is aligned with their strategy and do not waste time on activities that do not contribute to the ultimate goal. They are extremely efficient with their time and energy, making sure that every effort counts.

Strategy also includes building a strong team. Millionaires know they can't do everything alone, so they seek out the right people to help them implement their vision. They choose experts in different areas and trust them to handle specific tasks. This way, they can focus on what really matters: steering the overall direction of their business.

Finally, the strategy of millionaires always includes a focus on the future. They don't just think about next year, but about the next five, ten, or even twenty years. They consider how their current decisions will affect their business in the long term. For example, they may invest in technology or infrastructure today, even if they don't see immediate results, because they know that these elements will be key to their future growth.

The power of strategy lies in its ability to provide clarity and direction. While others feel lost or improvise along the way, millionaires move forward with confidence because they know exactly what they are doing and why they are doing it. Strategy not only allows them to achieve their goals, but it also gives them a competitive advantage, because while others are reacting, they are already two steps ahead. If you want to think like a millionaire, start planning every action, study your environment and make sure every decision is aligned with your vision. Remember, success is not accidental; it is the result of a well-executed strategy.

Creating Value, Not Just Profits

Creating value, not just profit, is at the heart of how millionaires think. They know that money is important, but it's not the only thing that matters. For them, profit is the natural result of creating something that truly makes a difference in people's lives. Instead of focusing only on how much they can make from a business, they ask themselves what problem they can solve, how they can improve a situation, or what unique experience they can offer. That value-added mindset is what leads them to build successful, long-lasting businesses.

When a millionaire starts a project, their first question is not "how much can I make," but "what need am I solving." They understand that money follows value, not the other way around. For example, if someone invents a product that makes life easier, people will be willing to pay for it. It's not just because the product exists, but because it provides something useful. Millionaires don't focus on selling something for the sake of selling it, but on offering something that people really want or need.

This doesn't mean that profits aren't important. In fact, they're essential to keeping a business running. But for millionaires, profits are a consequence of doing things right. It's like planting a tree: if you take care of the tree, water it, and protect it, it will eventually bear fruit. You can't focus only on the fruit without first taking care of the tree. Likewise, you can't focus only on profits without making sure your business provides real value.

A clear example of this is how millionaires view their customers. For them, customers are not just a source of money, but partners in their success. They try to deeply understand what their customers want and need. They ask questions, listen to their problems, and make sure their products or services are truly useful. When customers feel like they are receiving something valuable, they not only come back, but they also recommend the business to others. This creates a continuous growth effect that goes beyond any immediate profit.

Furthermore, millionaires understand that creating value is not just about the customer, but also about their employees and their community. A business that adds value takes care of its team, invests in their development, and treats them with respect. When employees feel valued, they work with more motivation and help the business grow. In the same way, millionaires look for ways to contribute to their community. They know that if they improve the environment in which they operate, they are also building a more favorable place for their business.

Creating value also means constantly innovating. Millionaires aren't content with doing the same thing as everyone else. They look for ways to improve what already exists or create something completely new. Innovation is a powerful way to add value because it offers solutions that weren't available before. Think about companies like those that have revolutionized technology or transportation. They succeeded because they didn't just focus on making money, but on how they could make things better for everyone.

Another important aspect is sustainability. For millionaires, creating value also means thinking about the future. They don't seek quick profits that harm the environment or exploit resources irresponsibly. They prefer to build businesses that can last for generations, because they understand that real value has no expiration date. This also helps them gain the loyalty of their customers, because more and more people prefer to support companies that care about more than just money.

Finally, creating value is not something that stops. Millionaires know that there is always more to do, more problems to solve, and more people to help. They never stop looking for ways to improve, grow, and contribute more. This not only benefits their businesses, but also gives them deep personal satisfaction. Knowing that they are making a difference in the world is a reward that goes beyond money.

If you want to think like a millionaire, start focusing on how you can create value in everything you do. Ask yourself what you can bring to the people around you, whether it's at work, in a business, or even in your personal life. Remember that money is a tool, but true success comes from doing something that leaves a positive mark. In the end, gains are temporary, but the value you create can last forever.

Negotiate Like a Master

Negotiating like a master is one of the most important skills a millionaire must master. Negotiation is not just a conversation where two people try to get what they want; it is an art, a strategy, and above all, an opportunity to build long-term relationships. Millionaires understand that successful negotiation does not mean "winning" at all costs, but rather finding an outcome where both parties are satisfied and willing to collaborate again in the future. This mindset is what makes them exceptional negotiators.

The first step to negotiating like a master is preparation. Millionaires never go into a negotiation uninformed. They thoroughly research the other party: who they are, what they want, what their needs are, and what their weaknesses might be. They are also clear about what they themselves want to achieve. They know what their ideal goal is, what the minimum acceptable goal is, and what they would be willing to sacrifice. Going into a negotiation unprepared is like going into battle without weapons: it simply doesn't work.

Another key is to listen more than they talk. Millionaires know that information is power, and the best way to get it is by letting the other person talk. When you listen carefully, you can identify what the other party really wants, even if they don't say it directly. Sometimes someone's true need isn't apparent at first, but if you pay attention, you can find ways to meet it in a way that benefits you, too. Listening also demonstrates respect and creates an environment of trust, which is crucial to a successful negotiation.

Clear communication is another key aspect. Millionaires don't use confusing words or try to manipulate with cheap tricks. They are direct and honest about what they want and what they are offering. This not only makes negotiation more efficient, but it also helps them build a reputation as trustworthy people. Once someone trusts you, they will be much more willing to come to an agreement that works for both of you.

It's also important to be flexible. Millionaires understand that a negotiation doesn't always go exactly as they planned.

While they have their goals clear, they are also willing to adapt if an unexpected opportunity arises or they face an obstacle. Flexibility doesn't mean giving in on everything, but rather being willing to explore creative options that can benefit both parties. This ability to think outside the box is what often gives them the upper hand in a negotiation.

Patience is another quality that millionaires bring to the table. They know that the best negotiations aren't hastily resolved. They're willing to take the time to analyze each offer and counteroffer, and they never let pressure lead them to make impulsive decisions. Instead of acting in haste, they focus on staying calm and carefully evaluating all possibilities. This calm approach not only helps them make better decisions, but it also gives them a psychological advantage, as the other party senses their confidence and security.

One tactic that many millionaires use is to focus on value, not just price. For example, if they are negotiating a contract, they don't just talk about the cost, but about everything they can offer in terms of quality, experience, and additional benefits. In this way, they turn the conversation into something broader than just discussing numbers. This approach allows them to demonstrate why their offer is more valuable, even if the price is higher.

Millionaires also know when it's time to walk away. Not every negotiation will end in a deal, and that's okay. The important thing is to recognize when a deal is simply not worth it. It may be because the terms are not favorable or because the other party is unwilling to cooperate. In those cases, walking away is not a failure, but a strategic decision. It's better to pass up an opportunity that could be detrimental in the long run than to accept a deal out of desperation.

Finally, millionaires always aim to leave a good impression at the end of the negotiation, no matter the outcome. Even if a deal doesn't come to fruition, they make sure the other party feels respected and valued. They never know when they might cross paths with that person in the future, and maintaining positive relationships is always a smart investment. Plus, closing on a positive note can leave the door open for future collaborations.

Negotiating like a master isn't something you learn overnight, but it's a skill that can be developed with practice and patience. If you want to negotiate like millionaires do, start by preparing well, listening more than you talk, being clear in your communication, and focusing on the value you can bring. Remember that a negotiation isn't a battle; it's an opportunity to build something together. In the end, the best negotiators are those who know how to create agreements that benefit everyone and strengthen long-term relationships.

Delegating and Building Elite Teams

Delegating and building elite teams is one of the most important strategies millionaires apply to achieve and maintain success. Although many start out as individuals solving problems and building businesses, at some point they realize they can't do it all on their own. The key to scaling any business or project is learning to delegate and surrounding yourself with highly capable people who not only share the vision but also bring complementary skills.

Delegation isn't just about telling someone else to do something. It's a skill that requires confidence, clarity, and planning. Millionaires don't see delegation as a way to get rid of boring tasks, but rather as a way to free up time to focus on the things that only they can do. For example, a successful entrepreneur knows to delegate tasks like daily administration or logistics to experts in those areas, while they focus on the bigger picture of the business or closing important deals.

The first step to delegating effectively is to identify tasks that can and should be done by other people. Millionaires make a list of everything they do in their day and analyze which of those activities really need their direct attention. Then, they look for someone who can not only do that task, but can probably do it better than they can. They aren't afraid to surround themselves with people who are more talented in specific areas because they understand that success is a team effort.

Once they find the right person for the job, millionaires are clear in communicating what they need. They explain the goal, the expected outcome, and any important details. They leave no room for confusion because they know that a lack of clarity can lead to costly mistakes. At the same time, they don't micromanage. They allow people to do their jobs in the way they find most efficient, as long as they meet the expected outcome. Not only does this lead to better results, but it also motivates team members by giving them autonomy and responsibility.

Building elite teams requires more than just hiring the people with the most impressive resumes. Millionaires look for people who align with their values, are committed to the business vision, and have a growth mindset. An elite team is not defined by technical skills alone, but by mindset. They know that a motivated, cohesive, results-oriented team is far more powerful than a group of talented but disconnected individuals.

Another thing that millionaires understand well is the importance of investing in their team. This doesn't just mean paying good salaries, but also providing them with tools, training, and opportunities to grow. When team members feel that they are being valued and that their development matters, they work with more passion and loyalty. Millionaires see their team as a long-term investment, not an expense. They know that a strong team can take their business much further than they could achieve alone.

Trust is another key pillar when building elite teams. Millionaires understand that for someone to give their best, they need to feel trusted. This doesn't mean being naive or letting serious mistakes slide, but rather giving people the space to prove their worth and learn from their mistakes. Trust breeds loyalty and fosters an environment where everyone is willing to go the extra mile because they know they are valued.

Finally, millionaires are aware that an elite team is not static. They are always looking for ways to improve, whether it is by bringing in new talent, developing current members, or adjusting team dynamics based on business needs. They also know when it is time to let go of someone who doesn't fit the group's vision or values. Although it can be a difficult decision, they prioritize the well-being and efficiency of the team as a whole.

At its core, delegating and building elite teams isn't just about handing out tasks or hiring the brightest people. It's about creating a culture of trust, commitment, and excellence. Millionaires know that their success depends not only on what they can do, but on what they can achieve with the support of a strong team. In the end, no empire is built alone, and the best leaders are those who know how to surround themselves with the right people to achieve extraordinary goals together.

Diversification

Diversification is one of the most important concepts that millionaires apply when building and protecting their wealth. In simple terms, diversifying means not putting all your eggs in one basket. It is a strategy that reduces risk by spreading resources across different areas, investments, or businesses. Not only does this protect your money in case something goes wrong, but it also opens the door to multiple sources of income and growth opportunities. Millionaires understand that the world of business and investing is uncertain, and diversification is their insurance against the unexpected.

The basic principle of diversification is to avoid dependence on a single source of income or a single industry. Millionaires know that things can change quickly in the market. A company that seems solid today could face unexpected problems tomorrow, or a booming industry could become obsolete in a few years. To protect themselves from these risks, they spread their money across different types of assets, such as real estate, stocks, bonds, their own companies, and in some cases, startups or emerging technology. Each of these sectors has its own characteristics and responds differently to changes in the economy.

A clear example is real estate investment. Millionaires don't just buy properties to live in, they also invest in income-generating properties, such as rentals or commercial projects. At the same time, they may have investments in the stock market, where they buy shares in companies that operate in completely different sectors, such as technology, healthcare or energy. This way, if one sector performs poorly, the losses can be offset by the returns from another sector.

However, diversification isn't just about randomly throwing money around. Millionaires carefully research each investment before committing. They study the risks, market trends, and growth opportunities. They also seek expert advice to make informed decisions. They understand that diversification doesn't completely eliminate risk, but it significantly reduces it by ensuring that not all of their investments are dependent on the same economic conditions.

Diversification also applies to business. Millionaires who run successful companies often branch out into other related or completely different areas. For example, an entrepreneur who owns a restaurant chain might decide to invest in agriculture to control the supply chain, or in technology to improve the customer experience. This diversification in business not only reduces risk, but also creates synergies that can benefit all areas of their company.

Another way millionaires diversify is internationally. They don't limit their investments or businesses to one country, because they know that local economies can be unstable. By investing in different international markets, they protect their wealth from economic problems specific to one region. Additionally, this allows them to take advantage of unique opportunities in other countries, such as emerging technologies, cheaper labor, or markets with less competition.

An interesting aspect of diversification is that it's not always just about money. Millionaires also diversify their time and energy. They understand that relying solely on one project or activity can be exhausting and risky. So, they seek to balance their time between different projects, hobbies, and relationships. This approach not only makes them more productive, but it also helps them stay motivated and open to new ideas.

It's important to note that diversification doesn't mean dispersion. Millionaires don't invest in everything that comes their way. They are selective and strategic. They analyze each opportunity to make sure it fits with their goals and risk tolerance. They also constantly monitor their investments and adjust their portfolio based on market conditions. If something isn't working anymore or a better opportunity comes along, they don't hesitate to change course.

In short, diversification is a strategy that every millionaire adopts to protect and grow their wealth. It's not just about spreading money around in different places, but doing so in a strategic and well-thought-out way. By distributing their resources across multiple areas, they reduce risk and increase their chances of success. Diversification is a lesson that we can all apply in our lives, even if we're not millionaires. Whether we're managing our money, our time, or our projects, having options and not relying on just one thing gives us stability and opens the doors to more opportunities.

Invisible Opportunities

Invisible opportunities are those that are right in front of everyone, but very few manage to see them. Millionaires have a special ability to detect them because they have trained their minds to look at the world differently. Where others see problems, they see solutions; where others see obstacles, they see alternative paths. This ability is not magic or an innate talent, but the result of an open mind, constant curiosity and the willingness to analyze things from a unique perspective.

To understand how to spot invisible opportunities, it's important to first understand why many people don't see them. Most of the time, we're so focused on what we do day to day that we don't stop to look at the bigger picture. We get used to accepting things as they are and don't question whether they could be different. Millionaires, on the other hand, are always asking questions: Why does this work this way? How could it be better? What problems are people facing that no one is solving? These questions are the starting point for finding opportunities that others overlook.

A common example of an invisible opportunity is identifying unmet needs in a market. Millionaires pay attention to people's feedback, complaints, and difficulties they face in their daily lives. These complaints are signs that something can be improved or created from scratch. For example, if they often hear that people are frustrated because delivery services are slow, they might consider creating a more efficient system. This approach requires not only listening, but also connecting the dots to see how to solve that problem profitably.

Another way to find unseen opportunities is to look at industries or markets that are growing or changing. Millionaires don't just look at what's working now, but at what could be important in the future. This requires being informed, reading, researching, and keeping an eye on trends. For example, before electric car technology exploded, some visionaries were already investing in it because they saw the long-term potential. These opportunities aren't always obvious at first, but those who spot them early are the ones who reap the biggest benefits.

Millionaires are also experts at identifying value in things that others find unattractive or irrelevant. For example, they may look at an old, neglected building and, instead of dismissing it, think about how they could renovate it and turn it into a profitable business. They may look at a struggling small business and wonder if, with a few changes, it could be transformed into a success. This ability to see potential where others see failure is what sets them apart.

It's also important to mention that invisible opportunities aren't always in completely new areas. Often, they're in improving something that already exists. For example, a popular product can be perfected, a service can be made more accessible, or an experience can be optimized for customers. Millionaires know that it's not always necessary to invent something from scratch; sometimes, it's enough to just make something better or more efficient.

Fear of risk is another factor that causes many people to fail to see invisible opportunities. Millionaires understand that every opportunity has some degree of uncertainty, but they don't let that stop them. Instead of fearing failure, they analyze risks in a calculated manner and make informed decisions. They know that even if they fail, each attempt teaches them something valuable that they can use in the future. This mindset drives them to explore ideas that others would shy away from for fear of making a mistake.

Finally, millionaires don't work alone in their search for opportunities. They often surround themselves with people with different perspectives and experiences. They know that an idea may seem invisible to one person, but obvious to another. Listening to others, collaborating, and sharing ideas can be the key to uncovering those hidden opportunities.

In short, invisible opportunities are everywhere, but they require a different mindset to be seen. It's about opening your eyes, asking questions, observing trends, listening to problems, and being willing to take calculated risks. Millionaires have learned that the world is full of possibilities for those who know how to look beyond the obvious. If you train your mind to think like them, you'll discover that the opportunities you seek have been right in front of you all along, waiting for someone to take advantage of them.

Adapting to Change

Adapting to change is one of the most important skills millionaires develop throughout their lives. The world is constantly changing, and nothing stays the same for long. Technology advances, markets change, customer preferences evolve, and new opportunities emerge while others disappear. Millionaires not only accept this reality, they embrace it as part of their strategy. They know that resisting change is a sure way to fall behind, while adapting to it is a way to stay relevant and successful.

Adapting to change doesn't simply mean reacting to what happens. For millionaires, it's about anticipating changes before they happen and preparing for them. This requires being informed and alert. For example, an entrepreneur who notices that online shopping is increasing exponentially won't wait for their brick-and-mortar business to lose customers. Instead, they'll look to integrate e-commerce before change negatively impacts them. This ability to stay ahead of the curve allows them to not only survive, but thrive in times of transformation.

Another way millionaires adapt to change is by accepting that failure is part of the process. Not every strategy works, and not every change brings instant positive results. But rather than seeing failure as an obstacle, they view it as an opportunity to learn and adjust their approach. For example, if a new marketing strategy doesn't produce the sales they expected, they don't persist with it out of pride. Instead, they analyze what went wrong, make the necessary adjustments, and try again with a better perspective. This mental flexibility allows them to move forward while others get stuck in their mistakes.

The ability to adapt to change also requires an open mindset. Millionaires don't hold on to old ideas or ways of doing things just because they worked for them in the past. They understand that what was effective yesterday may not be relevant tomorrow. This is especially evident in technology industries, where innovations emerge quickly and companies must constantly evolve to stay competitive. Even in more traditional businesses, a willingness to change can make the difference between success and failure. Millionaires are willing to let go of what no longer works and embrace new ideas, even though they may initially seem challenging.

Furthermore, millionaires don't see change as something they have to face alone. They recognize the importance of surrounding themselves with people who are also willing to evolve and learn. Their teams are made up of individuals who bring new perspectives and skills that complement their own. This allows them to approach changes from different angles and come up with innovative solutions. For example, an entrepreneur facing the transition to artificial intelligence will look to hire technology experts who can guide their company through the process, ensuring that the change is smooth and successful.

One of the keys to adapting to change is staying focused on the long-term purpose. Millionaires have a clear vision of what they want to achieve and understand that changes are just part of the journey toward that goal. This helps them stay on track when things get complicated. For example, an entrepreneur who wants to build a global brand may be faced with changes in international laws, economic fluctuations, or new consumer expectations. Instead of getting discouraged, they will adjust their strategy without losing sight of their main goal.

The fear of change is something that many feel, but millionaires deal with it differently. They don't see change as a threat, but rather as an opportunity to grow. They know that staying in their comfort zone can be tempting, but also limiting. So, although change can be uncomfortable at first, they accept it as an inevitable part of success. This attitude allows them to not only adapt, but also leverage change as a competitive advantage.

In short, adapting to change is an essential skill that separates millionaires from those who lag behind. It requires an open mindset, the ability to learn from failure, a willingness to let go of what no longer works, and a commitment to staying focused on long-term goals. Millionaires know that change is not something to be feared, but something to be embraced. In a constantly evolving world, those who adapt not only survive, but thrive. If you develop this skill, you will be better prepared to face any challenges that come your way to success.

Making Data-Driven Decisions

Making data-driven decisions is one of the most effective strategies millionaires use to build and maintain their success. Instead of relying solely on intuition or assumptions, they prefer to work with concrete, verifiable information that allows them to assess situations clearly. This doesn't mean that intuition has no place in business, but when combined with solid data, decisions are much more accurate and reliable.

The first step to making data-driven decisions is to gather relevant information. Millionaires don't make decisions blindly; they always seek to understand the bigger picture. For example, if they're considering launching a new product, they don't just go by their enthusiasm for the idea. Instead, they analyze the market, research demand, study the competition, and gather data on their customers' spending habits. The more data they have, the more informed their decision will be.

Once they have the data, the next step is to analyze it. This is where many fail, because collecting information is worthless if it is not interpreted correctly. Millionaires know how to find patterns and trends in numbers.

For example, if they are seeing a drop in sales, they don't just focus on the negative result. Instead, they investigate the causes behind that drop. They might discover that sales decline in certain seasons, that there are problems with distribution, or that customers prefer a competing product. This detailed analysis allows them to take specific steps to address the problem rather than making random changes.

Another important aspect of making data-driven decisions is measuring the impact of previous decisions. Millionaires don't just make a decision and leave it in the past; they always review the results to determine if it was the right one. If the data shows a strategy is working, they double down on it. If not, they analyze what went wrong and adjust their approach. This constant cycle of deciding, evaluating, and adjusting is what allows them to continually improve and stay ahead of the competition.

It's important to note that data doesn't always have to be complex or technical. Sometimes, the most useful information can be very simple. For example, a customer survey can reveal which aspects of a product need improvement. A social media analysis can show what type of content generates the most engagement. Even observing how customers behave in a physical store can provide valuable clues about how to optimize the layout of the space or the placement of products.

Another key point is that making data-driven decisions doesn't mean ignoring creativity. Millionaires know that data is a tool, not a constraint. Data provides them with a solid foundation on which they can build innovative ideas. For example, if an entrepreneur notices that their customers prefer more personalized options, they could use that information to develop a new service that combines personalization with advanced technology.

Technology has made it easier than ever to collect and analyze data. Millionaires are leveraging tools like data analytics, artificial intelligence, and business management platforms to make faster, better decisions. These tools not only allow them to see what's working in real time, but also to predict future trends. For example, an entrepreneur who uses predictive analytics can anticipate a surge in demand for a product and prepare to meet it before it happens.

However, it's also crucial not to become obsessed with data to the point of paralysis. Millionaires know that no data set is perfect, and that at some point, action must be taken. The key is to find a balance: collecting enough information to make an informed decision, but not so much that the drive to act is lost. They know that even with the best data, there will always be uncertainty, and being willing to take calculated risks is part of the process.

Finally, millionaires understand that data is a way to minimize errors, but not to eliminate them entirely. There will always be variables outside of their control, but by basing their decisions on concrete information, they significantly increase their chances of success. Plus, they know that every decision, whether good or bad, provides them with more data for the future. In this sense, constant learning is a fundamental part of their approach.

In short, data-driven decision making is a practice that allows millionaires to act more accurately, reduce risks, and maximize results. It's not about getting bogged down in numbers, but about using information strategically to make smart decisions. If you adopt this approach, you'll find that your decisions will have more impact and that you'll be better prepared to face the challenges of the business world.

Financial Discipline

Financial discipline is one of the fundamental pillars in the lives of millionaires. It is not just about making money, but how to manage it intelligently, consistently and strategically. People often believe that millionaires spend carelessly because they have large amounts of money, but the reality is completely different. Their wealth is not the result of luck or waste, but of careful planning and solid financial habits that they practice every day.

The first principle of financial discipline is to spend less than you earn. Although it seems simple, many people fail at this basic point. Millionaires understand that no matter how much money comes into their account, they must always keep some money to save and invest. They don't live to impress others with unnecessary luxuries; instead, they prioritize what truly adds value to their lives and businesses. For example, a successful entrepreneur can afford a luxury car, but if that car doesn't serve a specific purpose, they'd rather use that money to invest in something that will generate more income.

Another key aspect of financial discipline is keeping a close eye on income and expenses. Millionaires don't leave their finances to chance. They keep a precise record of how much they earn, what they spend it on, and how much they save. This habit not only allows them to know exactly where their money is, but it also helps them identify opportunities for improvement. For example, if they notice they're spending too much in an area that isn't essential, they make adjustments to redirect those resources toward something more productive.

Financial discipline also involves building an emergency fund. Millionaires know that life is full of unexpected events and that it is crucial to be prepared. This fund is not for investments or daily expenses, but to cover unexpected situations such as an economic crisis, a health problem or any other event that may affect their income flow. Having this backup gives them peace of mind and allows them to move forward without making hasty or risky decisions.

Millionaires also understand the importance of avoiding unnecessary debt.

It's not that they never use credit, but they do so strategically. For example, they might take out a loan to invest in an income-generating business, but they would never use credit to fund a lifestyle they can't afford. To them, debt is a tool to be carefully managed, not a shackle to their financial freedom.

Another common practice among millionaires is consistent investing. They don't keep all their money in savings accounts where it loses value over time due to inflation. Instead, they look for ways to make their money work for them. They invest in real estate, stocks, businesses, and other opportunities that will generate passive income. However, these investments aren't impulsive; they're backed by analysis and a deep understanding of the market. This is a form of discipline that requires patience and a long-term approach.

Financial discipline also extends to setting clear goals. Millionaires don't just save and invest without a defined purpose; they have specific goals they want to achieve. For example, they may set a goal of saving a certain amount to reinvest in their business or to secure their retirement. Having these goals gives them a sense of direction and helps them stay focused on their financial priorities.

One point that cannot be overlooked is that financial discipline does not mean being stingy. Millionaires understand the value of spending on what matters, whether it is education, life-enriching experiences, or charitable causes. They know that money is a tool, not an end in itself. This balanced mindset allows them to enjoy their success without losing sight of the importance of maintaining responsible management of their finances.

Financial discipline also requires a mindset shift. Many people view money as something that is out of their control, but millionaires understand that it is up to them to take control. This means continually educating themselves on financial issues, seeking advice when needed, and being willing to learn from mistakes. They don't get carried away by impulses or emotions when it comes to money; they always make decisions based on logic and facts.

Finally, financial discipline is a habit that is built over time. Millionaires are not born with this skill; they develop it through constant practice and self-discipline. They know that every little effort counts and that the habits they adopt today will have a significant impact on their financial future. This approach allows them to build and maintain their wealth sustainably, no matter what external circumstances.

In short, financial discipline is the foundation upon which millionaires build their success. It involves spending less than you earn, keeping tight control of income and expenses, avoiding unnecessary debt, investing wisely, and setting clear goals. It's a habit that requires commitment, but one that offers huge rewards in the long run. If you adopt this approach in your own life, you'll be on the right path to achieving financial stability and, over time, the financial success you desire.

Networking

Networking is one of the most powerful tools millionaires use to build their success. No matter how smart, hard-working, or talented you are, the connections you have can open doors that would otherwise remain closed. For millionaires, networking isn't just about attending events and handing out business cards; it's a deliberate strategy to create meaningful, mutually beneficial relationships.

The foundation of effective networking is understanding that it's not about you, it's about the other person. Millionaires know that the key to building strong relationships is to provide value before asking for something in return. For example, if they meet someone who can be helpful to their business, they don't start by asking for a favor. Instead, they look for ways to help that person first. It can be something as simple as introducing them to someone else they're interested in or sharing a useful resource. This approach builds a relationship of trust and reciprocity from the start.

Networking also requires getting out of your comfort zone. Many millionaires aren't naturally extroverted, but they understand that building a strong network is critical to their success. So they make a conscious effort to attend events, talk to new people, and stay in touch with those they already know. They don't wait for opportunities to come to them; they actively seek them out. This level of proactivity is what makes the difference between those who just accumulate contacts and those who build truly useful relationships.

An important lesson about networking is that quality always trumps quantity. Millionaires don't seek to amass thousands of superficial contacts. They prefer to have a smaller circle of people with whom they have a real connection and whom they can trust. For example, a successful entrepreneur may have only a handful of strategic partners, but they know that these relationships run deep and offer immense value both personally and professionally. This doesn't mean ignoring new connections, but rather focusing on nurturing the ones that really matter.

Following up is another crucial aspect of networking. It's not enough to meet someone once and assume you already have a relationship. Millionaires are very good at staying in touch with the people they meet. This doesn't mean constantly sending messages, but rather finding authentic ways to keep the relationship alive. They might send an email to congratulate someone on an accomplishment, share an article they think they might be interested in, or simply ask how they're doing. These small gestures create a lasting impression and strengthen the connection.

Another important point is that networking doesn't always happen at formal events. Millionaires understand that every interaction is an opportunity to connect. It can be on a plane, in a cafe, or even at a casual meeting. The important thing is to be open and ready to interact with new people at any time. This means actively listening, showing genuine interest, and being willing to share something about yourself.

Authenticity is an aspect that cannot be underestimated. Millionaires know that people can quickly detect when someone is only interested in what they can get from them. Because of this, they strive to be sincere in their interactions. Not only does this help them build stronger relationships, but it also gives them a reputation for integrity and trustworthiness, which is invaluable in the business world.

Furthermore, millionaires view networking as a long-term investment. They don't expect immediate results from every connection they make. They understand that some relationships can take months or even years to bear fruit. But when they invest time and effort into building a strong network, they know that opportunities will eventually appear. This patience is what differentiates those who view networking as a chore and those who view it as a life strategy.

Technology also plays a crucial role in modern networking. Millionaires use tools like LinkedIn, emails, and social media to stay in touch and expand their network. But even with all the technology available, they know that nothing replaces the power of a face-to-face conversation. That's why they always look to combine digital networking with personal networking, making sure to build relationships that are genuine and meaningful.

Finally, millionaires understand that networking is a two-way street. It's not just about receiving, but also about giving. They are willing to share their time, knowledge, and resources with others, not because they expect something in return right away, but because they know that helping others is a way to strengthen their network and reputation. This generous approach creates an ecosystem of mutual support where everyone can thrive.

In short, networking is much more than accumulating contacts. It is an ongoing process of building authentic relationships, providing value, and staying connected with the people who can positively impact your life and business. If you take this approach, you will not only have a stronger network, but you will also open doors to opportunities you never imagined. Networking, when done right, is not only a business strategy, but a way to enrich your life in every way.

Think Big, Act Small

Thinking big and acting small is a philosophy that millionaires apply to turn ambitious dreams into attainable realities. This mindset combines the vision of a grand future with the discipline of taking small daily steps that lead toward that goal. It's the formula that allows them to handle monumental projects without feeling overwhelmed, staying focused on what really matters.

Thinking big means not being limited by current circumstances. Millionaires visualize their success in bold ways. If they want to build a global company, they don't dwell on the resources they don't have now; instead, they focus on what they could achieve if they reach their full potential. This type of thinking leads them to imagine opportunities that others overlook, because they aren't afraid to dream big. For them, dreaming small is just as difficult as dreaming big, so they prefer to aim high.

But while they keep this broad vision, they also know that you can't achieve something huge in one leap. This is where acting small comes in. Acting small doesn't mean thinking narrowly, but breaking down a big goal into more manageable tasks. For example, if they want to build a company that makes millions, they don't start out trying to tackle everything at once. They focus first on building a solid product, then on getting their first customers, and then on scaling the business. Each action is designed to bring them one step closer to their big vision.

This combination of big thinking and small action also helps them manage risk. Imagine a millionaire has an idea for a revolutionary new product. Instead of investing all his resources straight away, he starts with a simple prototype to test whether the idea works. If it succeeds, he then invests more. This approach prevents them from wasting large amounts of money and energy on ideas that might not work, while allowing them to confidently move forward with those that have potential.

Another important aspect is that acting small encourages consistency. Sometimes, big goals can feel unattainable, and this leads many people to give up before they even start. Millionaires avoid this problem by focusing on daily actions. They know that they don't need to build an empire in a day, but they do need to do something every day that brings them closer to their goal. This habit of constant progress is what, over time, transforms small achievements into big results.

Thinking big and acting small also involves learning and adapting along the way. Millionaires understand that they don't have all the answers from the start. So as they pursue their goals, they use each step as an opportunity to learn. If something isn't working, they adjust their strategy. If something works, they expand it. This approach allows them to continually improve and ensure they're moving in the right direction.

A classic example of this philosophy is how many millionaires start their businesses from scratch. Instead of waiting to have everything perfect, they launch a basic version of their idea. It may not be the most impressive version, but it allows them to go to market, get feedback, and improve. This incremental process helps them get to their final vision without being paralyzed by perfection.

Furthermore, acting small doesn't mean thinking in terms of scarcity. Millionaires always have the mindset that every small action has the potential to multiply. An initial investment may seem modest, but if continually reinvested, it grows exponentially. This applies not only to money, but also to time, energy, and relationships. They know that what starts as a small step can set off a chain of events that takes them much further than they ever imagined.

It's also important to mention that this philosophy isn't just for business. Thinking big and acting small can be applied to any aspect of life. If someone wants to improve their health, they don't need to try to make radical changes overnight. They can start with something as simple as walking ten minutes a day or swapping an unhealthy meal for a more nutritious option. Over time, these small changes add up and make a significant impact.

Finally, millionaires know that thinking big and acting small requires patience. It's not a quick or easy path, but it's the most effective one. They accept that success doesn't happen overnight and are willing to work consistently to build something lasting. They understand that every small step counts, and that every action brings them one step closer to that big vision they have in mind.

In short, thinking big gives millionaires a clear and ambitious direction, while acting small allows them to move forward without feeling overwhelmed. It's a powerful combination that keeps them motivated, focused, and always making progress. If you adopt this mindset, you'll find that no goal is too big or dream too ambitious, as long as you're willing to start with small steps and keep moving forward each day.

Taking Advantage of Crises

Taking advantage of crises is a skill that sets millionaires apart from the rest. While most people see a crisis as an insurmountable problem, millionaires see it as a hidden opportunity, waiting to be discovered. They know that difficult times create chaos, but they also open doors that don't exist in times of stability. This mindset allows them to not only survive crises, but to emerge stronger and more successful than before.

The first step to taking advantage of a crisis is to stay calm. In uncertain situations, many people react with fear or impulsiveness, making decisions that make their situation worse. Millionaires understand that fear clouds judgment, so they focus on analyzing the situation clearly. They don't get carried away by the panic of the moment. Instead, they ask themselves key questions: What is changing? What problems need solutions? Where can I add value in this new context?

A clear example of this is how they react to economic downturns. While most people cut back on spending and seek safety, millionaires look for investment opportunities. They know that during a crisis, prices fall and assets that would normally be out of reach become more accessible. They buy properties, stocks or even businesses that are in trouble, with the view that these investments will grow in value once the economy recovers.

Another important aspect is that millionaires understand the power of adaptation. A crisis almost always brings changes in people's needs and behaviors. For example, during the pandemic, many traditional companies struggled to survive, while those that quickly adapted to the digital world thrived. Millionaires observe these trends and adjust their strategies to align with the new reality. They don't cling to what worked before; they are willing to reinvent themselves if necessary.

They also use crises to identify problems that need urgent solutions. They know that where there is a problem, there is an opportunity to offer a product or service that solves it. For example, during a health crisis, they might invest in medical technology or companies that manufacture essential supplies. During an energy crisis, they might explore alternative sources of energy. They see crises as a time to innovate and create, rather than lament the difficulties.

The crisis-taking mentality also involves acting quickly. Opportunities that arise in these moments don't last forever. Millionaires are prepared to move quickly when they identify an opportunity. This doesn't mean acting impulsively, but rather making informed decisions with agility. They understand that time is of the essence in a crisis, and that whoever acts first often reaps the greatest reward.

However, it's not all about external opportunities. Crises also offer an opportunity to reflect and strengthen foundations. Millionaires use these moments to evaluate their strategies, eliminate what doesn't work and reinforce what does. If a crisis exposes weaknesses in their business, they address them head-on, ensuring they are better prepared for the future. They don't see difficulties as failures, but as lessons they can use to improve.

Another key point is that millionaires see crises as a time to build relationships. During difficult times, many people look for support and guidance. Millionaires take advantage of this to establish genuine connections, helping others and forming strategic alliances. These relationships not only help them get through the crisis, but they also create opportunities for the future. They know that in times of greatest need, the strongest partnerships are built.

Taking advantage of a crisis also requires a long-term view. Millionaires don't focus solely on surviving the moment. They think about how the decisions they make now will benefit them in the years to come. For example, if they invest in a business during a crisis, they don't expect immediate results. They have the patience to wait for the market to recover and for their investment to reach its true potential.

It's important to note that taking advantage of a crisis doesn't mean ignoring the risks. Millionaires do careful analysis before acting. They assess the worst-case scenario and make sure they're prepared to deal with it. But unlike many, they don't let the fear of risk paralyze them. They understand that every great opportunity comes with some level of uncertainty, and they're willing to take calculated risks to reap significant rewards.

Finally, millionaires have the ability to inspire others during crises. While many lose hope, they transmit confidence and optimism. This leadership allows them not only to motivate themselves, but also to mobilize their teams, partners and even their clients. Crises, for them, are an opportunity to stand out and prove that they can overcome any challenge.

In short, seizing the benefits of crises is an art that combines vision, adaptation, and strategic action. Millionaires don't see tough times as an insurmountable obstacle, but as fertile ground for growth. They stay calm, identify opportunities, adapt quickly, and act decisively. It is this mindset that allows them to turn the most challenging times into the most profitable and meaningful of their lives. If you can adopt this perspective, you will find that even in the worst crises there are opportunities for success waiting to be seized.

Automated Systems for Financial Freedom

Automated systems are the path to financial freedom. Imagine a scenario where money keeps coming into your bank account, even while you sleep, travel, or just enjoy time with your family. This is the dream of many people, but for millionaires, it is a reality. This does not mean that they got there by magic. They achieved it by designing and using systems that work efficiently, with or without their constant intervention.

An automated system is nothing more than a set of processes that operate independently or with little oversight, generating consistent revenue. To understand this, think of a business that sells products online. Once the website is set up, customers can place orders, payments are automatically processed, and products are shipped without the owner having to manually intervene. This is an automated system in action. Millionaires don't just create these systems; they also fine-tune them to maximize their performance.

The first step in implementing an automated system is to identify repetitive tasks or key processes in a business or investment. Millionaires are experts at spotting areas where human time is being wasted unnecessarily. For example, if you run a sales business, you probably spend a lot of time managing inventory, processing orders, or answering frequently asked questions from customers. These are ideal tasks to automate using specialized software or tools.

Technology is the cornerstone of automated systems. Today, there are countless apps and programs designed to simplify almost every aspect of a business or investment. From platforms that manage social media to automated trading systems, the possibilities are endless. Millionaires invest time in learning about these tools, because they understand that every dollar spent on automation will save them hours of work in the future. This approach allows them to free up their time to focus on more strategic activities or to simply enjoy life.

Automation isn't limited to business, though. It can be applied to personal finances, too. For example, millionaires often set up automatic transfers to invest in index funds or real estate. This way, their money works for them constantly, without them having to make decisions every day. This takes the emotional factor out of the equation and ensures that their financial goals keep moving forward, even in times of distraction or crisis.

Another crucial aspect is delegation. While technological automation is powerful, not everything can be handled by a machine. Millionaires combine technology with human talent. They hire skilled people to oversee systems and troubleshoot when necessary. For example, an e-commerce business may use software to process orders, but a human team will be on hand to handle more complex issues or provide customer support in exceptional situations. This balance between automation and human oversight ensures that the system is efficient and reliable.

One of the biggest benefits of automated systems is that they eliminate the need to be physically present to generate income. This gives millionaires the freedom to live wherever they want and do whatever they want with their time. Some travel the world, others focus on creating new businesses or projects, and some simply enjoy the peace of mind that comes from knowing their financial future is secure. The freedom these systems offer is priceless, and that is why millionaires value them so much.

But not everything is perfect. Creating and maintaining an automated system requires an initial investment, both in time and money. Millionaires don't skimp on these resources because they know the return will be exponential. They also understand that systems aren't static; they need to be constantly updated and optimized to adapt to changes in the market or technology. This continuous improvement mindset is what ensures that systems remain profitable in the long run.

Furthermore, millionaires are aware of the risks of automation. They know that relying entirely on an unsupervised system can be dangerous. For example, a bug in automated trading software could cause significant losses in a matter of minutes. That's why they always implement regular monitoring and checks to make sure everything is working as it should. This preventative approach minimizes risks and ensures that systems work for you, not against you.

A common mistake many people make when trying to automate is trying to do everything at once. Millionaires, on the other hand, approach automation gradually. They start with the simplest processes and optimize them before moving on to more complex tasks. This phased approach allows them to build robust, effective systems without becoming overwhelmed or making costly mistakes.

Ultimately, automated systems don't just make money; they also make peace of mind. Knowing that your financial future doesn't depend solely on your personal time or effort is a liberating feeling. Millionaires understand that money isn't the only valuable resource; time is even more valuable. And by automating, they're buying time—time to think, time to enjoy, and time to build a legacy.

In short, automated systems are one of the most powerful keys to achieving financial freedom. Millionaires use them to multiply their income, free up their time, and reduce the stress associated with day-to-day business or investment management. It's not an instant or easy process, but the results are worth it. If you're willing to invest in technology, delegate, and learn, you can create systems that work for you, opening the doors to a freer and more financially stable life.

Legacy as the Ultimate Goal

For millionaires, legacy is much more than just a fancy word. It is the purpose that gives meaning to all the effort, decisions and investments they make throughout their lives. Building a legacy means leaving something that transcends, that impacts other people even when they are no longer around. It is not just about accumulating wealth, but about creating a lasting impact that reflects their values, their achievements and their vision of the world.

Legacy can take many forms. For some, it is a carefully managed fortune that ensures the financial stability of their families for generations. Others prefer to contribute to social causes, build foundations or fund projects that improve people's lives. Some millionaires see their legacy in the companies they have built, which can continue to operate and provide employment and value to society long after they have retired. Regardless of the form, the concept is the same: leaving something meaningful behind.

A key aspect of legacy is that it requires conscious planning. It is not built by accident or in a haphazard way. Millionaires think long-term and make strategic decisions to ensure that what they leave behind has a positive impact and is sustainable. This includes everything from choosing investments to how they raise their children. They want to ensure that their legacy not only survives, but thrives.

One of the areas where legacy is most reflected is in the family. Many millionaires strive to pass on not only their wealth, but also their values. They want their children and grandchildren to learn how to manage money responsibly, work hard, and contribute to society. They don't want their heirs to simply spend money senselessly, but to use it as a tool to build something even greater. That's why they dedicate time and resources to teaching the next generation about the importance of effort, discipline, and generosity.

But legacy is not limited to the family sphere. Millionaires also seek to impact their communities and the world. Many of them use their wealth to fund hospitals, schools, research projects or cultural initiatives. They understand that money has a transformative power and want to use it to make a difference. This type of legacy not only benefits others, but also gives them a deep sense of purpose and personal fulfillment.

Building a legacy isn't easy, though. It requires sacrifice, discipline, and a clear vision. Millionaires know that in order to leave something meaningful behind, they must first forgo immediate gratification. This means investing in long-term projects, even when the results aren't immediately visible. It also means making tough decisions, like prioritizing certain goals over others or facing criticism for their actions. But for them, the effort is worth it, because they're working toward something bigger than themselves.

Another important aspect of legacy is sustainability. Millionaires don't want what they build to disappear quickly. So they spend time structuring their businesses, foundations, or investments so that they can operate efficiently and profitably in the future. This may involve setting up trusts, selecting competent leaders, or implementing systems that ensure continuity. In this way, they ensure that their legacy will last beyond their time.

Legacy is also about emotional impact. It's not just about what they leave behind materially, but how they inspire others. Many millionaires consider their greatest legacy to be not the money they accumulate, but the lives they touch. This can include employees they've helped grow, communities they've transformed, or even the ideas they've shared that have changed the way others see the world. This type of legacy is intangible, but deeply valuable.

It's important to note that legacy isn't something that only millionaires can build. Anyone can work to leave something meaningful behind. However, millionaires have the advantage of having resources that allow them to amplify their impact. This gives them an added responsibility, because they know they have the power to influence the world in ways that others can't. Many take this responsibility seriously and make it a central part of their lives.

Ultimately, legacy is not just a goal, but an ongoing process. Millionaires don't wait until they are at the end of their lives to start building it. They do it every day, with every decision they make. Every investment, every conversation, every project is a piece of the puzzle of their legacy. And while the end result may not be fully visible while they are alive, they are confident that what they are doing will have a lasting impact.

In short, legacy as an ultimate goal is much more than an accumulation of wealth. It is the expression of who they are, what they value, and how they want to be remembered. Millionaires understand that their true success is not measured in dollars alone, but in the impact they leave on people and the world. They work hard not only for what they can enjoy in the present, but for what they can build for the future. And in that effort, they find a purpose that goes beyond any amount of money.

9 7 9 8 2 3 0 5 6 9 3 5 0